Why Emerging Markets Will Recover Faster Than Developed Economies After the Next Global Financial Crisis

To gain some perspective into what's happening today, one can simply look back at the Asian financial crisis of 1997 when dollar funding dried up for countries like Thailand, South Korea, Malaysia and Indonesia. When those countries were running enormous current account deficits, the economic theory pundits from the IMF and the US Treasury vehemently opposed money printing in response to the crisis, warning against a collapse such as the one Zimbabwe faced in the years following that.

Asian countries took the advice and didn't print money which resulted in banks going bust, companies collapsing, unemployment rising and then a recession ensued. However, the economic, financial and political catastrophe in some ways created a sort of laxative effect because with the economic slowdown, current-account deficits disappeared and balances swung back into surplus, which brought on the much needed rains of recovery as central banks were gradually able to start cutting rates again and the gloom was replaced with sunshine and rainbows.

During the financial crisis of 2008 on the other hand, the world stood witness as western governments and central banks implemented the measures which they had previously advised Asian economies against. The Federal Reserve Bank, European Central Bank, Bank of Japan, Bank of England and the Swiss National Bank all began printing money.

Interestingly, when central banks printed money they bought bonds with those proceeds. Now we have a situation where for example, the ECB has bought so many bonds. The Swiss National Bank has been a big buyer of German government bonds, noticeably intervening to try and prevent the Swiss franc going up. To the point where now, we have negative yields on bonds. We have the Swiss 10-year government bond yielding almost -1 percent and the Swiss 50-year bond at a negative yield to maturity.

Why is it important to highlight these developments?

The most significant contrast to draw today between the emerging world and the developing world is that the approach to economic and monetary policy in the emerging world is still broadly orthodox compared to western economies that are now running unwonted economic and monetary policies.

Ironically, it's the west that is now on the cliff edge. The crisis developing in the west is financial and increasingly becoming economic. This leaves room to assume that it will at some point in the future turn into a wider social and political problem. So when considering risk, it is not unreasonable to assume that emerging markets are somewhat safer havens when compared to the developed world which appears to be more at risk.

If the US yield curve is right and the inversion of 2-10 years in the treasury market is the harbinger of the next recession, which it has been every time historically, then been central banks in the west have very limited firepower today to respond to economic weakness. There really are no more bullets left in the gun or at least very few. They've fired all the bullets. Interest rates are near zero. They have already massively expanded central bank balance sheets. So what do they do if they go into recession? It's safe to assume that they have already reached the limit of the modern monetary theory experiment in the west. The reason I subscribe to this notion is simply the fact that significant damage has already been caused to individuals, banks, pension funds and insurance companies.

Most people in the west don't earn any interest on their savings anymore. And when you consider that banks make money when interest rates are high, yield curves are steep, and credit spreads are wide and you have the opposite of all those three conditions in the world at the moment, especially in Europe, it spells disaster.

If you look at the share prices of the major European banks, they are simply unflattering.

This is unsustainable because these banks cannot make money in a negative yielding environment, where yield curves are flat and credit spreads are so tight. To give a clearer picture, consider pension funds, particularly in Europe. For example, you have a fund with billions in Swiss francs of assets, but with the 10-year Swiss government bond at minus 50 basis points, it's hard to determine what your liabilities are because you can't discount by a negative risk free rate since it's mathematically impossible.

The unrealistic risk mitigation strategy in such a case would be making a suggestion to the board of the pension fund to take all the money out of negative yielding bonds and hold physical bank notes in a bank vault so that you can pay pensioners with physical cash because at least physical cash maintains its value in nominal terms.

Pension funds around the world are seeing a massive increase in their liabilities because long-term yields have come down. For example, just recently in August 2019, the 30-year treasury broke below 2 percent. Moreover, you have insurance companies globally that have this incredible mismatch between the yield of the assets that they can go out and buy today and the value of the liabilities which were set when yields and interest rates were much higher.

The only people who made any meaningful wealth gains in the last decade are the 1 percent of the 1 percent. The elite who hold equities but of course there is this huge bubble in the stock market and 99.9 percent of the population have been left behind. If you consider traditional portfolio theory, what has been the role of government bonds in portfolios? It has been the asset class that makes money when risky assets fall off.

In 1998, when equities fell, those with bonds did really well because bond prices went up and equities went down. And yes, those who rebalanced their portfolios and sold out of their bonds and bought equities at every bump along the road over the last 20 or 30 years have done incredibly well. But up to this point most bubbles that have burst were not in supposedly risk-free assets. In 1998 it was emerging markets, in 2007 it was credit markets, in 1987 it was the stock market, in 2000 it was tech. But what the west has never had to cope with before is a bubble in the risk-free asset class. So what happens when that goes pop! What's the new risk-free?

Emerging markets better equipped to respond proactively in the next global financial crisis?

In an environment where the west finally wakes up, it's going to impact everybody including emerging markets. But in that type of environment, relatively speaking, emerging markets will likely perform better. The reason for this is that emerging markets will be better equipped to respond more proactively. They'll be able to do that because emerging market balance sheets are far stronger than the balance sheets of the developed world.

Let's take the United States for example, a lot of people focus on the debt in the US. It is awash with debt. The government debt is out of control, students are up to their ears in debt and corporate America is the most highly leveraged it has ever been. Corporate America is more highly leveraged today than it was in 2007 and in the US bond markets, there is 3 trillion dollars of corporate debt sitting at triple B.

Now, the US high-yield market is only one trillion dollars. If some of these very highly leveraged triple B names are faced with an economic slowdown and their business models go kaput, then they are going to start sliding into double B territory. And the question we have to ask is: who is going to buy all this newly high-yielding debt? One trillion dollars of new high-yield debt just doesn't go into an existing one trillion-dollar bond market. It simply doesn't make sense. It has to massively reprice and of course as it reprices, it further blows up this highly leveraged model.

But debt isn't the problem in the United States, it's liabilities. According to **usdebtclock.org**, US unfunded liabilities are over 125 trillion dollars. What does that mean to the man on the street? Well, what that means is that the US government has promised to pay people for healthcare, unemployment, social security, etc. They've made promises to pay people 125 trillion dollars but they haven't funded it. Where is the US government going to get 125 trillion dollars from? There is no way on earth they can pay this money to the people to whom they owe it in terms of a currency that is worth no more than toilet paper. It simply cannot be done and that's the problem!

What could end up taking place is a situation where you'll see unrest building up around who gets the claims that the US government can manage to pay. This is a recipe for disaster. It could trigger civil war. This view is not far-fetched as arguably civil war is already breaking out in America at the moment. If you are black, brown, yellow, a woman, gay or if you're Muslim, you are already under attack in America. It's happening and it's very sad.

Society is breaking down. There is sensational leadership in the US government, brexit in Europe and you have the UK government making similar promises that Americans have made to their people. Promises that they cannot possibly keep. Italy has already threatened to leave the European Union. The west looking more like a basket case at this point.

And then you have China. People get very worried about a country like China. What's the essential difference between China and the west? One is political. In China there is no political cycle. President Xi Jinping will likely lead for a very long time. There is very little doubt about that unless he falls under the proverbial bus.

The difference between the Chinese government and the American government is that the Chinese government is solvent. The reason why they are solvent is that they have very low levels of debt. Secondly, they have very low levels of liability and thirdly, they have an asset-packed balance sheet. In China you have state-owned enterprises which are massively profitable and the big banks in China turn out massive profits. Governments in Asia and governments in emerging markets seem to have very sound economic and monetary policies in comparison to the west which is heading down the Zimbabwe School of Economics path.

It is very worrying. The west is verging on a catastrophe and what's more interesting is that the markets are just beginning to wake up to this and we are beginning to see a rise in volatility.

If you consider what western central banks have done over the last decade since the global financial crisis, it looks like they have been playing a game whack-a-mole with volatility. Every time volatility has spiked up, they've managed to hit on the head by some combination of cutting interest rates and/or printing money.

More worrying is the possibility that if they have another spike up in volatility, banks might not be able to continue playing this game of whack-a-mole. The concern comes with recognising that they cannot continue to play the game indefinitely because they are at the end of the game.

If they do come out with another bout of quantitative easing, then banks are going to go bust. Pension funds are going to go bust, and insurance companies are also going to go bust. If quantitative easing inflates the stock market back up again then the 99.9 percent of the population are probably not going to tolerate more handouts to the 0.01 and 0.001 percent.

This means that there could be serious social and political instability. The west is at the point where they need to wake up to this reality and seeing as they are already on the top of the rollercoaster looking down. Perhaps that's why they continue to keep their blindfolds on because it will most likely be a pretty scary ride down. Emerging markets are not immune. They will also be hit hard but they will most probably recover faster since they at least have some ability to do so.

THE END

Note to reader:

I am not an economist or financial expert. This book was inspired by analysis and comments made by other subject matter experts. I take no credit for the ideas, theories and perspectives explored. I merely put my learnings derived from their content to present the thoughts and ideas in a readable and relatable format with a view to address the question or line of thought posed in the book's title.

Sources:

https://www.livewiremarkets.com/wires/the-developed-world-is-on-the-brink-of-a-financial-economic-social-and-political-crisis

https://www.usdebtclock.org/

Recommended reading:

https://www.theguardian.com/business/2019/apr/11/serious-threat-emerging-economies-us-recession-china

https://www.economist.com/leaders/2018/10/11/the-next-recession

https://www.lazardassetmanagement.com/us/en_us/research-insights/outlooks/Emerging-Markets.html

https://www.imf.org/external/pubs/ft/wp/2010/wp10237.pdf

https://www.newstatesman.com/politics/economy/2019/03/next-crash-why-world-unprepared-economic-dangers-ahead

https://www.imf.org/external/np/pp/eng/2010/061510.pdf

https://voxeu.org/article/resilience-emerging-markets-during-global-crisis

https://www.worldbank.org/en/publication/global-economic-prospects

http://www.ifre.com/a-history-of-the-past-40-years-in-financial-crises/21102949.fullarticle

https://www.thestar.com.my/business/business-news/2018/09/03/will-emerging-markets-rise-on-us-recession

https://www.forbes.com/sites/jessecolombo/2019/06/30/current-u-s-recession-odds-are-the-same-as-during-the-big-short-heyday/

https://economictimes.indiatimes.com/markets/stocks/news/emerging-markets-dont-sweat-that-yield-curve-yet/articleshow/68555390.cms?from=mdr

https://www.bloomberg.com/opinion/articles/2019-03-24/will-emerging-markets-retreat-after-u-s-yield-curve-inverted

https://www.nytimes.com/2019/08/12/upshot/august-financial-troubles-history.html

https://www.theguardian.com/business/2019/apr/11/serious-threat-emerging-economies-us-recession-china

https://www.worldfinancialreview.com/the-predicted-2020-global-recession/

https://personal.vanguard.com/pdf/icrgr.pdf

https://www.schwab.com/resource-center/insights/content/market-perspective

https://www.thecapitalideas.com/articles/guide-to-recessions

https://www.odi.org/blogs/10680-africa-10-years-after-global-financial-crisis-what-we-ve-learned

http://www.frbsf.org/economic-research/files/Goldstein_Xie.pdf

https://www.ft.com/content/d95e1d14-b727-11e8-bbc3-ccd7de085ffe

https://www.barrons.com/articles/emerging-markets-contagion-risks-on-the-rise-1536173998

https://journals.openedition.org/poldev/144

https://nationalinterest.org/feature/pending-emerging-markets-economic-crisis-31272

THANK YOU FOR READING